Original title:
The Lyrical Launchpad

Copyright © 2025 Creative Arts Management OÜ
All rights reserved.

Author: Oliver Bennett
ISBN HARDBACK: 978-1-80567-868-7
ISBN PAPERBACK: 978-1-80567-989-9

Floating on Fragments

In a boat made of socks, I row with delight,
Chasing lost dreams that take to the flight.
My captain's a cat, with a hat far too wide,
We sail through the skies on a banana-shaped tide.

The jellyfish play tunes on a tuba so grand,
While octopuses dance with a full rock band.
A parade of lost marbles spins wildly around,
As laughter erupts from the depths of the sound.

Sailing on whimsy, we zigzag and zoom,
Hiccups erupt like a confetti-filled room.
Each wave brings a giggle, a twist, and a twirl,
In a sea made of candy, we laugh and we swirl.

So raise up your spoons, toast the joy that we find,
In a world full of madness, let silliness bind.
On this floating adventure, we won't miss a beat,
Come join the fun ride—life's a humorous treat!

Flights of Rhyme

In a world where nonsense flies,
A penguin sings under sunny skies.
With socks that dance and shoes that giggle,
We twirl and tumble, doing a wiggle.

A cat in a hat throws a pie,
While jellybeans bounce oh so high.
We toast with juice, then slip and slide,
In this quirky place where laughs abide.

Gossamer Horizons

Marshmallow clouds float in the air,
While chickens tap dance without a care.
With crayons that whisper funny jokes,
We twirl like tops, surrounded by folks.

A squirrel rides bikes with a grin so wide,
As goofy giraffes take a silly glide.
We gather our giggles, stack them in piles,
And launch them off with a wave of smiles.

Notes Adrift in Time

A clock with legs skips through the room,
Singing songs that make kittens zoom.
We float on tunes like bubbles in air,
And sprinkle our laughter, everywhere.

The saxophone's laughing, it plays a note,
While silly frogs wear their silly coat.
We waltz with merriment, light as a feather,
Creating a symphony, never to tether.

Breezes of Metaphor

In gardens where puns bloom like flowers,
We dance on the breeze for hours and hours.
With words that tickle like soft feathers,
We bounce on laughter, dancing together.

A fish on a bicycle takes a ride,
And elephants play hide-and-seek with pride.
With giggles that echo and joy that shines,
We float to the rhythm of nonsensical lines.

Chords of Altitude

Guitars strum high in the sky,
With clouds as our audience, oh my!
Birds are dancing to tunes so bright,
While we play on, a comical sight.

Balloons join in, they're quite the crowd,
With every note, they drift and proud.
A symphony of giggles and cheer,
As we launch our melodies near.

Harmony of Heights

In a treehouse made of dreams,
We orchestrate ridiculous themes.
Laughter echoes, a playful tune,
As squirrels join in under the moon.

With popcorn clouds as our stage set,
Each high note brings a new duet.
We reach for stars, the skies applaud,
As hummed harmonies make us nod.

Updrafts of Inspiration

Kites soar high, with tails so long,
They join in on our silly song.
A gust of wind, and up they go,
Chasing dreams, like children in tow.

Inspiration floats, just like a kite,
Tickling our fancy, oh what a sight!
With giggles and glee, we chase the breeze,
Creating a whirl of joyous tease.

Sonorous Skylines

The city hums with bubbly notes,
As rooftops dance in wobbly boats.
Friends on sidewalks break into song,
With every step, they can't go wrong.

A trumpet toots, a saxophone squeals,
Neighbors laugh, spinning their wheels.
In this skyline filled with fun,
We find our rhythm, second to none.

Echoes of Imagination

In a world where dreams take flight,
Cats wear hats and dance at night.
Balloons float high with silly tunes,
And cows play chess under the moons.

A toaster sings when bread gets brown,
Pigs in pajamas prance around town.
Socks with holes have tales to share,
As unicorns laugh without a care.

Verses from the Launchpad

The rocket's top is made of cheese,
As space mice fly on cosmic breeze.
Planets twirl in polka-dot dresses,
While comets tell their funny messes.

Aliens dance at interstellar bars,
Serving drinks in mason jars.
Their jokes are weird but full of glee,
As they sip stardust by the sea.

Starlit Journeys

Sailing ships with seagull crews,
Navigate through rainbow hues.
The captain's hat? A cake surprise,
With jellybeans as the prize.

They giggle on the waves of light,
As fish in ties take flight at night.
Each splash a joke, each wave a pun,
With laughter echoing, oh what fun!

Songs of Celestial Ascent

A bubble choir sings today's hits,
While raindrops dance in joyous fits.
The moon hums tunes of silly lore,
As sparkling stars tell jokes galore.

With comets swirling in a line,
They prance and twirl, a grand design.
Galaxies laugh, twinkling bright,
In the vastness of the cosmic night.

Poetic Propel

In dreams we fly on paper planes,
With rhymes and giggles, joy remains.
Bubbles burst, we take a leap,
Where silly verses dance and creep.

A cat in boots begins to sing,
While frogs in hats do fiddling.
We laugh at clouds that wear a frown,
As words take off and spin around.

Journeys in the Skyline

A monkey swings on words so bold,
With tales of treasure, stories told.
Up on clouds, we drink some tea,
While ducks in ties chant harmonies.

An ant in shades rolls on a slide,
As rhymes like rockets soar and glide.
With every wink and twist of fate,
We orbit laughter, never late.

Serenade for the Stars

Stars in bow ties throw a bash,
With meteors dressed in glitter and flash.
Jokes that twinkle, puns that shine,
Here's to laughter in the sky divine!

A comet runs, it trips, it falls,
It tickles Saturn, through the halls.
But don't you fret if it gets lost,
For in this fun, it's worth the cost.

Ephemeral Elevation

A riddle floats like cotton candy,
With smirks and winks, oh so dandy.
We twirl through dreams on rainbows bright,
With giggles echoing through the night.

Dancing through clouds and silly jokes,
With wise old owls and marshmallow folks.
Up we go, on laughter's wing,
In a world where mirth is king.

Chasing Celestial Chords

In a world where music flies,
We chase the stars with silly sighs.
A kazoo here, a tuba there,
All the while we dance in air.

With rubber ducks that honk and squeak,
We serenade the moon's pale cheek.
A tambourine that's lost its jingle,
But still we laugh and start to mingle.

Jelly beans in every note,
Shooting stars, we start to gloat.
As rhythms bounce beyond our grasp,
We giggle loud, and need to gasp.

So let the symphony begin,
With goofy grins and hearts akin.
We'll launch our tunes to greet the night,
In a cosmic jam that's pure delight.

Ethereal Elevation

Up we float on clouds of cheese,
With every giggle, every sneeze.
The notes take flight like birds in jest,
In this high tune, we're truly blessed.

Our voices echo, a bubble burst,
In rhythms zany, we all thirst.
With silly hats and twirling moves,
In space, we glide, where laughter grooves.

The moon looks down, she joins the fun,
With sparkly dance and rays to run.
A symphony of giggles high,
We reach for stars, oh my, oh my!

Ethereal tunes, a silly tune,
We'll rattle on till late afternoon.
With bubbles poppin' in the air,
Our laughter dances everywhere.

Skyward Serenades

On blue balloons, we sail so high,
Singing songs that make us cry.
But they're tears of laughter, you see,
As harmonies rise, wild and free.

With trumpet plants that hum a tune,
We waltz beneath the watchful moon.
Bananas on guitars don't fret,
In this sweet madness, we forget.

Clouds play pianos, soft and grand,
As we jiggle-jump in merry band.
A wobbly world of joyful spree,
In every note, pure jubilee.

So join the choir of painted skies,
Where every note is made of pies.
With each crescendo, we just laugh,
In our ensemble, we find our path.

Wings of Whimsy

With rainbow wings, we take our flight,
Through giggles filled with sheer delight.
The sky is painted with our dreams,
As silly laughter bursts at seams.

We twist and twirl in dizzying spins,
With music made from jelly sins.
A chorus line of bouncing frogs,
Sings serenades to passing dogs.

The sun joins in, a playful grin,
As we parade with grins and spins.
Oh, what a sight, this jolly crew,
With melodies that paint skies blue.

So let the whimsy guide our way,
As tunes bring color to the day.
With every note, we'll spread our cheer,
In this bright world, we have no fear.

Whispers of Dawn

A rooster crows, thinks he's a star,
But still can't find his own guitar.
The sun peeks in with a cheeky grin,
While sleepy cats plot their next spin.

Toast pops up like a cannonball,
Burnt on edge, it's the breakfast brawl.
Butter slides like a sneaky thief,
While jam decides to cause a beef.

Harmonies in Orbit

Two squirrels singing in a high tree,
Who knew they had such harmony?
One plays a nut, the other a leaf,
Their concert's full of comic relief.

Aliens tuning into Earth's weird sound,
Wondering why humans twist around.
They laugh at dances that make no sense,
And misinterpret the world's pretense.

Flight of Fancy

A parrot dreams of piloting space,
While wearing goggles with a comical grace.
He squawks at planets like they're his pals,
And plays tag with misfit cosmic gals.

In dreams he finds a rocket so blue,
Made of bubblegum, as bright as dew.
He zooms past stars with a twisty laugh,
Writing his name on the Milky Path.

Beyond the Blue Horizon

Beyond the hills, where goats wear hats,
A field of daisies dances with chats.
The butterflies gossip, winged delight,
About a line that cut the sky tight.

In a kite's tail, there's a squeaky mouse,
Dreaming of cheese in a tiny house.
Clouds giggle as they float on by,
While a dreamer wonders, "How high can I fly?"

Aviary of Artistry

In a tree of colors bright,
Birds of every hue take flight.
Chirping tales of afternoon,
Painting skies with a joyful tune.

Feathers fluffy and full of zest,
Each one claims to be the best.
A pigeon boasts of its plumage fair,
While a parrot sings without a care.

Sparrows giggle at a squirrel's dance,
As robins try to take their chance.
A canvas forms in playful bursts,
Nature's art, it certainly thirsts.

So grab a brush, let laughter flow,
In this aviary, art steals the show.
With every chirp, a masterpiece grows,
In this funny place where creativity glows.

Sonic Sojourns

Whistling winds and playful sounds,
Dancing notes swirl all around.
A trumpet cat of orange hue,
Plays jazz with a groovy view.

Trombones slide on a bumpy ride,
Bass guitars thump with feline pride.
Each sound a giggle, a waggish jest,
In this concert, chaos is best.

The speaker's leap, a bouncy beat,
Echoes are tricky on the street.
With headphones on, a llama sways,
Grooving funny through the days.

So come and join this merry crew,
Let music lift your spirits anew.
Sonic leaps on this silly stage,
Laughter wraps around each page.

Wings of Whispers

In the hush of twilight's grace,
Soft whispers play a game with space.
A butterfly flips and flutters by,
Telling secrets as it flies high.

A moth wears glasses, vintage flair,
While ladybugs gossip without a care.
Shapes of shadows, tales unfurl,
Imagine a snail in a twirl!

Silly once, wise yet quick,
Ants in line do a rhythmic trick.
Whispers unveil an artist's muse,
In laughter's riddle, we choose to cruise.

So sneak a peek and take delight,
In this world, a whimsical sight.
With wings to giggle, mirth is near,
In every whisper, joy will cheer!

Ethereal Echoes

In the mist, where shadows play,
Echoes bounce in a quirky way.
A ghost with bubbles starts to float,
Sipping laughter from a giddy moat.

The moon wears a crown made of cheese,
While stars giggle in a cosmic breeze.
Jokes ricochet through the night,
Creating ripples of sheer delight.

A comet twirls with comical grace,
Tickling planets in a cosmic race.
These echoes spin with joyous cheer,
In a universe that holds us dear.

So hop aboard this laughter train,
Through ethereal echoes, fun remains.
With smiles and chuckles, soar on high,
Underneath this cosmic sky!

Skylark Sonnet

A skylark sings with all its might,
Flapping around on a sunny height.
It tells of socks found on the floor,
And laughs at cats that sleep and snore.

It dives for crumbs, avoids the rain,
With wings that tickle, never pain.
It teases clouds, gives them a poke,
Then does a dance and cracks a joke.

Its chirps are silly, never bland,
A feathered fool, the best in the land.
In skies so blue, it hops and plays,
Forget your worries, enjoy the days.

So come and join this feathered spree,
Where laughter echoes, wild and free.
No serious notes, just silly tunes,
With skylarks dancing under moons.

Ascent into Poetry

I climbed a hill where rhymes were born,
With clumsy steps, my shoes were torn.
The words were bouncing, full of glee,
    Like jelly beans on a rickety spree.

There were poets perched upon the sky,
In funny hats, they waved goodbye.
With candy pens and paper trails,
They penned their dreams and goofy tales.

Each stanza giggled as I passed,
In comical forms, so unsurpassed.
They danced with commas, twirled with glee,
In this odd world where rhymes run free.

So here's my wish for you today,
To find the joy in what you say.
Let laughter guide your words so bright,
    As you ascend to newfound heights.

Celestial Words

The stars aligned in silly ways,
With space cats dancing, giving praise.
They wrote in cosmic, twinkling ink,
Making jokes, you'd never think.

A moonbeam slipped on banana peels,
While asteroids played at spin the reels.
Galaxies laughed in spiral dances,
Sharing secrets in goofy glances.

A comet zoomed with bells that rang,
It juggled planets, and then it sang.
Oh, what a sight, this wondrous show,
Of jokes that glitter and laughs that glow.

So when you gaze at the night sky bright,
Remember laughter in its flight.
For every twinkle, a giggle's hid,
In the cosmos vast, where humor's bid.

Luminous Lines

With luminous lines, we scribble fate,
A touch of whimsy, never too straight.
They twist and turn, like dizzy sprites,
    Spreading joy on chilly nights.

Our words are wiggly, jumpy, and bold,
    Like playful puppies, never too old.
Each phrase a tickle, each dot a grin,
    In this bright world, let magic begin.

We write about muffins with hats made of cheese,
    And dancing pairs of runaway keys.
Each stanza sparkles, each verse ignites,
    With laughter soaring to dizzying heights.

So grab your pen, let humor flow,
In luminous lines, we steal the show.
Let chuckles bubble, let giggles rhyme,
For poetry's fun, every single time.

Soaring Verses

With a jig and a joke, we take to the sky,
Words like confetti, they scatter and fly.
Rhyme on a rocket, we giggle and zoom,
Chasing our dreams, like cats with a broom.

Silly stanzas bounce off the clouds,
Tickling the sun, in our fluffy shrouds.
A laugh in our pocket, we dance on the breeze,
Poems like peanuts, they're sure to appease.

Echoes of Inspiration

Bouncing ideas like a rubber ball,
Laughter erupts, as we rise and we fall.
Whispers of whimsy flutter through trees,
Silly sounds echo, carried by the breeze.

Words twirl and twist, like a playful kite,
Chasing the moon, in the soft, silver light.
Every chuckle, a new star in sight,
Sprinkling the cosmos, with glee and delight.

Flight of the Imagination

Up in the air, with a splash of delight,
We're painting the sky with laughter so bright.
Jokes are our jet fuel, as we soar through the blue,
Every line takes off, as if it just flew.

Imagination's a balloon, full of hot air,
Drifting through dreams, without a single care.
Riding the wind, where humor prevails,
Casting away doubts, like old, tattered sails.

Dreamscapes

In realms of absurdity, we frolic and sing,
Riding the coattails of funny old spring.
Witty wishes flutter, like butterflies bright,
A cascade of laughter, bringing pure delight.

With each little giggle, we spill out our dreams,
Sailing through clouds, on whimsical streams.
Joy wrapped in verses, a treasure to find,
Tickling our fancy, unconfined and unlined.

Horizons

From the peak of nonsense, we party and cheer,
Chasing horizons, where humor is near.
Every horizon whispers a cheeky line,
Inviting us all to taste pure sunshine.

A quip and a quirk, flying high and free,
Laughter like rain, sweet as can be.
The sunset chuckles, as we make our stand,
With giggles as our guide, let's make humor grand.

Whispers of the Sky

In a world where clouds wear hats,
Birds debate on silly chats.
Rainbows giggle, colors blend,
As moonbeams twist and dance, my friend.

Silly stars play hide and seek,
While comets laugh, so bold, so cheek!
Winds blow tunes that make you sway,
What a joy, in skies we play!

Kites fly high with little tails,
Tickling dreams as laughter sails.
Chasing joy from here to there,
Skyward wishes float in air.

Sunsets paint with crayons bright,
And shadows dance, oh what a sight!
In a world where fun takes flight,
Come join the whimsy, pure delight!

Infinite Resonance

The echo of a giggle spreads,
Bouncing 'round on silly threads.
Each ripple in the air we weave,
A symphony of joy, believe!

Laughter bubbles, never ends,
As we tease and joke like friends.
A pun flies by, a jest, a wink,
In this space, we laugh and think.

Notes of chuckles fill the night,
Melodies of sheer delight.
In every silly sound we make,
Waves of fun, oh make no mistake!

Twinkling tunes in funny lore,
With every note, we want some more.
So join the chorus, sing along,
In this place where we're all strong!

Cascading Words

Words tumble down like a waterfall,
Silly phrases, catch them all!
Puns and jests like butterflies,
Flapping wings in wondrous skies.

Chatter flows like rivers bright,
In this chat, we laugh tonight.
With every twist and every turn,
A new delight that we all learn.

Giggles bounce in endless streams,
While rhyme races on moonbeams.
Catch the words as they cascade,
In this fun, our fears will fade.

Fables spun with twists and turns,
In goofy tales, our heart still yearns.
So toss your worries to the breeze,
In laughter's flow, we find our ease!

Voyage to the Unknown

Grab your hat, let's take a ride,
In a boat where giggles glide.
Off we sail, both far and wide,
To lands where silly dreams reside.

Monkeys dance on bouncing waves,
Telling tales that our heart craves.
From laughter's shores to ticklish lands,
Adventure grows in funny bands.

Oceans sing with voices bright,
While dolphins join, what a sight!
Pirates jest, with treasure maps,
Full of jokes, and funny traps!

Wonders wait beyond the sea,
In every twist, joyful glee.
So hoist the sails, come share the fun,
On this voyage, joy has begun!

Wings of Expression

When words take flight like clumsy birds,
They flap about, ignoring the herds.
With a giggle, they soar, unrefined,
Painting giggles in the clouds they find.

A pun drops down, it lands with a splat,
It wiggles and jigs, now look at that!
In this wild chase of wit and jest,
Every flight becomes a lyrical quest.

Metaphors hang like laundry on a line,
Dancing in the breeze, oh isn't it fine?
With every slip and little faux pas,
The joy of expression becomes a bazaar.

So strap on those wings, don't be afraid,
Embrace the chaos, let fun invade.
For in this world of playful delight,
Laughter and words take off in flight.

Celestial Compositions

In a sky where verses spiral and flow,
Stars chuckle as rhymes begin to glow.
With giggles that echo beyond the moon,
Gravity's grip makes them bounce like a balloon.

Sonnets that swirl in a cosmic dance,
Leap like meteors, taking their chance.
Each comet a pun with a sparkle of glee,
Creating a ruckus in the galaxy.

The planets all chuckle, oh what a sight,
As stanzas collide in the heat of the night.
With witty remarks that orbit and spin,
A symphony of humor begins to begin.

So grab your quill, take aim at the stars,
Let laughter launch you beyond cosmic bars.
Compose a tune with a twist in the end,
In this grand universe, let joy be your friend.

Heights of Harmony

In the mountains of laughter, echoes resound,
Where melodies tickle and joy knows no bound.
Each note a chuckle, each chord a delight,
Harmonies frolic in the soft moonlight.

Riffs twist like gardens, blooming with cheer,
Tickling the senses, ringing in the ear.
As echoes bounce back, words dance and jive,
Creating a symphony that's oh-so-alive.

With every crescendo, giggles take flight,
Mountains of harmony, a wild delight.
The breezes whistle jokes, nature's own jest,
At such heights of joy, who could protest?

So tune your heart to this whimsical band,
Join in the laughter; take a bold stand.
For in this highland of joyous refrain,
Harmony blossoms, breaking all chains.

Incandescent Imagery

In a gallery where colors burst wide,
Paintbrushes giggle as they take a ride.
Each stroke hilariously splashes about,
Creating a visual symphony, no doubt.

Textures twist and turn in a playful way,
As canvas tickles, like jokes in a play.
With shades of silly humor, bright and bold,
This artful arena is a sight to behold.

A sculpture of laughter sits proudly on high,
Mimicking faces that seem to fly by.
Every twist tells a tale, quirky and fun,
As light paints the scene, where smiles are spun.

So step into this world of radiant cheer,
Where imagination rules without any fear.
For in this vibrant realm of imaginative spree,
The joyful creations come to life, just like glee.

Cadence of the Cosmos

In a rocket made of whimsy, we zoom,
Through candy clouds and laughter's room.
The stars play tag, we shout with glee,
While moonbeams dance, just you and me.

Galactic giggles fill the air,
Space squirrels juggling without a care.
As planets spin like tops so wide,
We drift in joy, our worries inside.

Shooting stars are winking bright,
Making wishes in the night.
With every twist in the cosmic game,
We bounce around, but who's to blame?

So pack your dreams and hold on tight,
We'll ride the waves of silly flight.
For in this universe made of cheer,
We're the jesters of the atmosphere.

Stratospheric Stanzas

On a trampoline of rhymes, we soar,
Bouncing high, we beg for more.
With every line, the laughter blooms,
Floating in joy like helium balloons.

The clouds are cotton candy sweet,
As we dance to the comet's beat.
Inverting gravity with a twist,
Who knew a verse could feel like bliss?

Doodles whirl like planets round,
In our sketchbook, silliness found.
Our words are rockets, bright and loud,
We scribble dreams above the crowd.

So let's leap into the zany sky,
With taglines that will make us cry.
Each stanza's a share, a joyous play,
Where chuckles echo all the way.

Uplifted by Verse

Verse by verse, we rise in glee,
On metaphors that set us free.
With giggles etching lines in space,
We bounce on rhymes, a silly chase.

Our thoughts are balloons, floating high,
Tickling the clouds as we fly by.
In the breeze of words, we sway,
Every syllable a fun-filled play.

With punchlines echoing through the void,
Laughter is the joy we've employed.
Catch a comet, ride it with flair,
This rocket of humor, beyond compare.

So join the fun on this wild ride,
Where puns and laughs can't be denied.
With every launch, a chuckle's near,
We'll soar through verses, year after year.

Astral Aspirations

In a rocket made of dreams and quips,
We sail through space on giggling slips.
With cosmic jokes and smiles abound,
Each moment twinkles, laughter's sound.

Above the world, our whims take flight,
Spinning tales beneath the starlit night.
In this gallery of interstellar cheer,
The universe hums, 'We're glad you're here!'

Every comet's trail holds a joke,
While lunar bunnies dance and poke.
With rhyming schemes like shooting stars,
We'll paste our joy on Saturn's bars.

So lift your spirit, join the fun,
In this playful race, we've just begun.
For in this vast and wacky quest,
We'll find our laughter, the very best!

Notes from the Ether

In the sky where giggles float,
Silly sounds in a musical boat.
A wink from the clouds, a chuckle divine,
Whimsical whispers, a dance on the line.

Jokes like confetti fall from above,
Tickling each heart, it's laughter we love.
With every note, a feather takes flight,
In this playful realm, the world feels just right.

Strings of joy in the stratosphere,
Creating a melody only we hear.
Bubbles of humor, they pop and they sing,
In the ether of giggles, our spirits take wing.

So let us gather, where humor will soar,
In this space of delight, come open the door.
Every glance shared, brings smiles all around,
In this sky of good cheer, joy is unbound.

Ascending Stanzas

Words like balloons start to drift high,
Up toward the sun, painting jokes in the sky.
Each line a rocket, fueled by our glee,
Shooting for laughter, so wild and so free.

Verses take flight on a breeze made of rhyme,
Giggling at gravity, defying all time.
In space made of chuckles, we leap and we bound,
A playground of puns where fun must abound.

With each silly line, our spirits grow bold,
Chasing the giggles, a treasure untold.
Stanzas like comets, they blaze a bright trail,
In orbit of laughter, we dance without fail.

So let's rise up high, to the sky we'll ascend,
With each twist of humor, and each little bend.
A flight of pure joy, together we'll sing,
In the realm of the funny, a magical fling.

Gliding Through Silence

In a quiet that tickles, we softly glide,
Echoes of laughter, like bubbles, collide.
Whispers of fun float, in the air all around,
In a hush filled with giggles, joy is unbound.

Dancing through silence, we twirl in delight,
With invisible wings, we swoop left and right.
Each giggle a ripple, a soft gentle tease,
As we glide through this space, with humor to please.

The stillness is silly, a slow-motion game,
In the quiet's embrace, no two are the same.
With each muffled chuckle, we float without care,
Gliding through silence, we're light as the air.

So join in the fun as we slip and we slide,
In the soft, silent moments where laughter can ride.
With cheeky grins shared, we create a bright scene,
In the calmness of joy, a whimsical dream.

Aflight on the Breeze

Catch a ride on the wind, let's take to the skies,
With humor as our wings, we're destined to rise.
Floating on laughter, we drift and we sway,
In a ballet of jokes, we dance through the day.

Each gust a snicker, each breeze a hooray,
With tickles and giggles, we soar far away.
A flight full of whimsy, in a world of delight,
With smiles as our compass, we'll follow the light.

In the air, we're weightless, with stardust to share,
Sailing on punchlines, we float without care.
A twist and a turn, with giggles that please,
A whimsical journey, aflame on the breeze.

So let's laugh through the clouds, with joy as our guide,
On this voyage of fun, let's travel with pride.
Together we'll wander, our spirits set free,
In this flight of pure fun, where we're meant to be.

Dreamweaving Journeys

In the land of socks and shoes,
The clouds can dance and snooze,
Bubblegum trees, oh what a sight,
I swear they giggle in the light.

With every step, a bouncing tune,
We ride on carrots to the moon,
As jellybeans rain from the sky,
We catch them quick, oh my oh my!

An octopus wearing a top hat,
Plays chess with a curious cat,
Each move is met with wisely laughs,
While cupcakes race in bubble baths.

So let's don our hats, both funny and tall,
And waltz like bubbles while having a ball,
In dreamweaving journeys, we spin and we sway,
With giggles and whimsy, we dance our own way.

Aetherial Expressions

Chasing rainbows on pogo sticks,
We juggle stars and silly tricks,
With each bounce, we soar above,
In a world that sparkles with joy and love.

Puppies in tutus twirl around,
Squirrels breakdance upon the ground,
Each feathered friend joins in with glee,
As we paint the skies, a jubilee!

Tickling clouds with laughter bright,
While unicorns prance with pure delight,
Every corner's filled with cheer,
In these aetherial dreams, we steer.

So grab your silly hats and let's ignite,
Expressions of joy that feel just right,
Together we'll frolic, dance, and play,
In a whimsical world that's here to stay.

Nimbus Narratives

Fluffy clouds serve pancakes wide,
As rainbows swirl, they cannot hide,
In this tale, sprinkles rain down,
A whimsical feast in a starry town.

Sailboats made of candy canes,
Float on rivers of fizzy grains,
Where gummy bears in capes take flight,
With laughter ringing through the night.

Lions wearing glasses read the news,
While frogs in tuxedos share their views,
Each tale unfolds with a merry twist,
In nimbus narratives, don't dare to miss!

So grab a woolly hat, take a seat,
As funny stories mingle and meet,
In this cloud-clad world, there's much to see,
Where laughter and joy run wild and free.

Celestial Choreography

Stars play hopscotch in the night,
While comets twirl with all their might,
Galaxies spin in a funky groove,
As planets gather, they get in the move.

Moonbeams bounce and shimmy with flair,
While asteroids join the cosmic fair,
They dance through space, in twinkling light,
Creating rhythms that feel just right.

Aliens joke in their whimsical way,
While shooting stars bright upstage the day,
Each pirouette leads to echoes of fun,
In celestial ballet, we're never done.

So twirl and twist amongst the glow,
Join the dance, let your spirit flow,
In cosmic choreography, laughter persists,
In this starry realm, we've made our tryst.

Skylines and Dreamlines

In a city where pigeons plot,
They aim for the crumb, give it all they've got.
A seagull swoops down, king of the scene,
While a squirrel debates whether to join the cuisine.

The skyscrapers chuckle, they rise with pride,
Watching the chaos, they cannot hide.
Hot dog vendors dance, ketchup in hand,
As mustard will surely make a brave stand.

A dog on a leash plays tug with a cat,
As onlookers laugh, 'What is up with that?'
The clouds roll in, playing tag with the sun,
In this land of goofy, absurdity's fun.

With a jazz band playing off-key in the park,
A frog leaps in rhythm, oh, what a lark!
Stay grounded, they say, but the laughter will rise,
Every mishap is magic beneath these bright skies.

Rhythms of the Ether

Through space and time, we all try to groove,
A comet spins wildly, just trying to move.
Aliens chuckle, their ships made of cheese,
Sharing odd jokes on the interstellar breeze.

Lightning bugs conduct in a dazzling light,
While stars do the tango, twinkling at night.
Planets align for a cosmic parade,
As Saturn wears rings that are never quite made.

Galaxies swirl in a perpetual tease,
As astronauts try dancing with cakes made of peas.
Meteors race like they're late for a show,
And laughter erupts wherever they go.

On radio waves, the echoes delight,
Every frequency dancing, what a strange sight.
While comets do the cha-cha with style,
This party in space surely goes on for miles.

The Art of Soaring

High above mountains where eagles do play,
A chicken once dared to fly far away.
With feathers unfurled and a heart full of cheer,
"Why can't I glide?" she proclaimed with a sneer.

As balloons floated by in a whimsical race,
The chicken took flight, at her own funny pace.
She flapped and she flopped through the light summer air,
While the owls and the doves looked on in despair.

A goose joined the madness, honking with glee,
They practiced their moves atop the big tree.
With a twist and a twirl, a monumental sight,
They danced through the clouds, oh, what pure delight!

With a gust of the wind, they buckled with laughter,
As the clouds kept on shifting, chasing thereafter.
So lemons were thrown, and pie in the sky,
For being a chicken, oh, now watch her fly!

Ascendant Echoes

In caverns of giggles where echoes collide,
A frog leaps for joy, and a snail takes a ride.
With echoes of laughter that bounce off the walls,
We'll sing silly songs until nighttime calls.

A penguin parades with a big rubber band,
Jumping and flapping, he sure is quite grand.
While shadows are dancing, they twist and they spin,
The moon starts to giggle, with a twinkle and grin.

Through portals of sound, the chimes they do chime,
In a whimsical world where humor is prime.
Float high on the vibes of a ticklish breeze,
Where all of our worries dissolve with such ease.

So join in the chorus, let all spirits lift,
In this festival of echoes, the perfect gift.
We'll bounce on the clouds, with joy we'll proclaim,
In every reflection, there's fun in the game!

Rhythms of the Undiscovered

In a world where socks can dance,
And teapots sing in a merry trance,
Pigeons wear hats made of cheese,
While cats play chess high in the trees.

Balloons float off to find their fate,
Chasing dreams at a snail's rate,
Hopping frogs recite funny laws,
As chickens offer a round of applause.

A fish in a hat throws a fishy bash,
With jellybeans making a joyful splash,
Mice in tuxedos hold hands and twirl,
As laughter's the currency of this swirl.

The moon does the cha-cha, shining bright,
While turtles tango in the newfound light,
Every giggle, a rhythm, bold and clear,
We dance through the night, no worries, no fear.

Celestial Serenades

Shooting stars hum a quirky tune,
While comets juggle beneath the moon,
Space cows play chess on a cosmic board,
And nebulae wear capes, never bored.

Galaxies giggle in spiral curls,
As asteroids throw glittering pearls,
Mars makes cupcakes with sprinkles and zest,
For laughter's the thing that's truly the best.

Stars don hats made of candy floss,
While planets debate who's the real boss,
In this playground where silliness reigns,
The universe dances, unanchored by chains.

Comets take selfies in the night sky,
While planets pop popcorn, oh my, oh my!
Every twinkle tells a tale untold,
In this realm where joy's pure gold.

Skylines of Emotion

The clouds wear hats of purple and green,
As rainbows play hopscotch, looking keen,
Birds in bowties sing with flair,
While kites tumble down without a care.

Sunshine does cartwheels, bright and bold,
While raindrops laugh, never cold,
A skyline made of giggles and dreams,
Where nothing is quite what it seems.

Trees sway to a funky beat,
As the breeze adds rhythm to their feet,
Squirrels wear shades, looking oh-so-cool,
In this vivid, wacky, nature school.

Laughter echoes from each painted beam,
While clouds conspire to burst at the seam,
Every hue a giggle, every shadow a sigh,
In this playground, let your heart fly.

A Symphony of Possibilities

In a world where spoons can play the drums,
And toaster pastries dance like happy chums,
Marshmallows frolic in the sunlight's glow,
While jellybeans congregate in a row.

Guitars made of cupcakes strum sweet tunes,
As jellyfish wear tiny silver spoons,
Every note's a burst of glee,
In this oddball orchestra, you see.

The saxophone croons, a lippy delight,
While violins tickle the air with fright,
Each sound is a giggle wrapped up tight,
In this symphony of silly flight.

Balloons escape with whimsical grace,
As harmonicas join in the embrace,
With every cackle, the laughter grows,
In a symphony where anything goes.

Poetic Anthems

In a world of rhymes and cheers,
Words dance around like lively dears.
Everyone joins in the silly parade,
With giggles and guffaws, let joy cascade.

Verses hop on a jumpy ride,
With puns and laughs, they can't hide.
Like a chicken that's learned to sing,
This anthem of fun makes the heart swing.

With every quip and pun so bright,
We celebrate under the moonlight.
A comical tune, oh what a feat,
These poetic anthems can't be beat!

So grab a friend and share the glee,
In a dance-off with a bumblebee.
For laughter is the best of arts,
Let's raise our voices, and connect our hearts.

Samba of the Skies

Up in the air, where the cowbirds sing,
Clouds twirl about, giving each a swing.
A penguin in shorts joins the crazy flow,
Samba beats pounding, it's quite the show.

Kites do the cha-cha in a breezy jam,
Hats flying off like a disco clam.
With every gust, we giggle and sway,
Who knew the wind could dance this way?

Jellybeans rain, like confetti from space,
As toucans join in with their own grace.
The sun shines brightly, a smile so wide,
In this samba of skies, let's take a ride!

So lift your wings, let's fly and twirl,
Laughing and spinning in a bright swirl.
Salsa with stars, break into a cheer,
This sky-high samba is truly dear.

Horizons of Harmony

On the edge of the world, where laughter flares,
We find silly secrets in quirky snares.
A frog in a tux, croaks operatic tunes,
While turtles play chess under crescent moons.

Strumming the banjo, a raccoon named Lou,
Sings ballads of mischief, much to our view.
With every strum, the audience glows,
In horizons of harmony, silliness flows.

Jam sessions erupt on a sunny day,
With sunflowers nodding along the way.
The ants in their hats dance beneath the sun,
In a world where laughter is always fun.

So gather 'round, let's make some noise,
In this patch of joy, everyone enjoys.
Bring your quirks and flares, join the spree,
In horizons of harmony, let's be free!

Cadence of Clouds

Clouds march by in a fluffy parade,
With giggling gales, they're never afraid.
Windy whispers and chuckles collide,
As raindrops slip on their slippery ride.

A cat in a hat floats on by,
Sipping lemonade, oh me, oh my!
With every poof, a new joke's unfurled,
In this cadence, watch as laughter twirled.

Puffy castles and raucous delight,
Playful banter fills the bright light.
Dancing shadows on the grass below,
In the cadence of clouds, let joy overflow.

So sing with the breeze, let troubles go,
With every tickle, let your heart glow.
For the clouds are our friends, oh can't you see?
In this world of laughter, we're all simply free!

Stellar Stories

In a galaxy far, they munch on cheese,
Aliens giggle, floating with ease.
Their dance, a wobble, quite out of line,
Chasing their tails, oh, isn't that fine?

Rockets made of candy, colorful beams,
Shooting through space, fulfilling their dreams.
With laughter and joy, they soar and swoop,
Creating a party, a cosmic hoopla group!

Stars twinkle brightly, a disco ball,
While comets join in for a lively hall.
Each tale outrageous, with whimsy in tow,
Echoing joy as they giggle and glow.

So join in the fun on this wondrous ride,
Where silliness sparkles, and pets are supplied.
Their stories of laughter, a treat for the night,
In the universe's warmth, everything's right!

Poised for Flight

Countless balloons float ready to burst,
Eager to launch, they're near to the first.
With snickers and giggles, a parade in the sky,
A trampoline cat gives a bounce and a sigh.

A penguin in goggles, quite keen for the show,
Practices dives from a high-flying blow.
With pies made of space cream and gravity pulls,
They leap with delight, dodging nonsense-filled ghouls.

Wobbling like jelly, the whole crew ascends,
Each giggle erupts, as the timeline bends.
The giggle-gravity forms a wobbly dance,
As giggles and joy make a whimsical chance.

So tether your creativity, raise your glass high,
With laughter and silliness, let's prepare to fly.
Unleash your bravado, let the fun ignite,
In this quirky ballet, all will be alright!

Canvas of the Cosmos

A canvas unfurls, painted with grace,
With splatters of stardust, it fills up the space.
Giggles and hue, a comical blend,
Like a cat with a paintbrush, this art will transcend.

Bizarre shapes appear, a purple dog floats,
On paint-splattered spaceships, they dance like goofy goats.
Swirls of confetti and pizza galore,
Unlikely creations we've never seen before.

The brush strokes of laughter echo through night,
As crayons of joy create pure delight.
With a sprinkle of humor, let colors collide,
In this playful cosmos, let laughter abide.

So come grab a brush, let your worries out,
Create with abandon, fill up the spout.
In the art of the stars, let your spirit reside,
With every stroke, let your laughter be cried!

Celestial Chants

In starry night skies, a chorus begins,
With cackles and croons, as the universe spins.
A choir of planets, with glee in their tone,
Sings silly ballads, in harmony grown.

Jupiter jiggles with laughter so merry,
While Mars adds a beat with its bouncy hit cherry.
Venus spins around, wearing socks and a hat,
As giggles erupt from a twinkling bat.

Comets are trumpets, shooting so bright,
With cosmic lyrics that spark pure delight.
Galaxies twirl as they laugh and they cheer,
Creating a concert, with joy ringing clear.

So grab your confetti, and dance in your shoes,
Join the cosmic party, with whimsical blues.
For when laughter resounds in this heavenly trap,
The universe joins in, with a giggling clap!

Crescendo of Dreams

In a world where wishes greet,
Silly dances move your feet.
Balloons float up to the sky,
While giggles echo nearby.

Tickle the clouds with a grin,
Jokes take off, let laughter spin.
Dreams collide like stars at night,
A comedy that feels so light.

Onward we soar, a wacky flight,
Chasing thoughts that feel so bright.
Every twist brings a surprise,
Admiring stars with laughing eyes.

So let your mind take off and play,
In this dance of dreams today.
With every note that tickles the air,
Life's funny tune, a joyful affair.

Chasing Cosmic Currents

Surfing through the trails of space,
Jelly-like stars in a funny race.
Spaceships made of candy bars,
Zooming by the laughing jars.

Galactic giggles fill the void,
While cosmic pies are deployed.
Asteroids dance, a wild affair,
Wobbling paths without a care.

Planets prank with silly spin,
Tickling moons that twirl and grin.
In this universe of play,
Every comet sings hooray!

So catch the waves of laughter's call,
As we ride the currents, one and all.
With every loop, we find delight,
In chasing stars, so bold, so bright.

Melodies in Motion

Jumping tunes play hide and seek,
Bouncing beats that giggle and peek.
A whirl of sound, a merry spin,
Where silly notes begin to grin.

Harmonies do the cha-cha-slide,
A dance of rhythms, step inside.
Ticklish strings and echoing drums,
Spin a web where laughter comes.

Music flows like jelly beans,
Squeaky shoes in funny scenes.
Every strum, a shout of glee,
Melodies race, come sing with me!

So let the music set us free,
In tunes where all can laugh with glee.
A playful art, a joyful motion,
Songs are mixed with pure devotion.

Symphony of the Stars

Underneath the twinkling light,
Stars conduct with pure delight.
Each wink a note, each glow a laugh,
Crafting jokes from a cosmic staff.

Shooting stars play peek-a-boo,
While moonbeams wear a funny shoe.
They harmonize through the night's embrace,
A silly, bright celestial space.

Constellations hum a soothing cheer,
Comets join in, spreading joy near.
With every twirl, the universe beams,
Creating giggles in hopeful dreams.

So come and join this stellar song,
Where laughter and music both belong.
In this symphony, find your heart,
For every night is a merry art.

Bubbles of Bliss

Frogs in hats jump high,
Sipping tea from the sky.
They dance on giant spoons,
To the laughter of the moons.

A cat in shades, oh so cool,
Plays chess on a wobbly stool.
While chickens sing rhymes,
To the sound of jolly chimes.

Rubber ducks in a parade,
Doing somersaults, unafraid.
Bubbles rise with a pop,
As giggles never stop.

In a land of snickers and fun,
Where jellybeans dance in the sun.
Each verse, a tickle, a jest,
In this world, we're truly blessed.

Quantum Quatrains

Socks that vanish in a blink,
Turn up blue with a wink.
While clocks run backwards, oh dear,
Time trips over, filled with cheer.

The universe laughs in delight,
As robots moonwalk at night.
Silly shapes twist and shout,
Worms wear crowns, there's no doubt.

Sauntering stars in a line,
Debating the taste of moonshine.
A comet trips, oh what a scene,
Sparkling like a jellybean.

With every quatrain, a giggle,
In this cosmos, we wiggle.
Dancing particles, such a show,
Let's launch into fun, let's go!

Euphonic Explorations

Whales in tutus sing a tune,
As ants play jazz beneath the moon.
A picnic on the ocean floor,
With sandwiches that can't be sore.

Bananas strum on ukuleles,
As gumdrops sway like happy melees.
Cupcakes chase the frosty breeze,
While jelly rolls down with ease.

In treasure maps made of candy,
Pirates dance, all quite dandy.
With laughter echoing through the days,
In a syrupy sunbeam's rays.

The world spins in sweet surprise,
Where giggles under the sky rise.
Let's play a tune on silly strings,
In this realm where joy takes wing.

Vistas of Verse

Kites shaped like flying pies,
Swirl with laughter in the skies.
Turtles rollerblade around,
In this playful, crazy town.

Celery sticks tell jokes wise,
As marshmallows fly, oh what a prize!
Unicorns on pogo sticks,
Performing all their greatest tricks.

Toasters toast with silly beats,
While spaghetti dances on its feet.
In worlds where whimsy is the core,
Every moment opens new doors.

Verses flutter, light as air,
Filled with giggles everywhere.
In this vast and wacky spree,
We find the funny, wild, and free.

A Canvas of Dreams

In a world where laughter blooms,
Pants turn into colorful costumes.
Brushes dance like silly clowns,
Painting smiles, erasing frowns.

Dreams flutter like butterflies,
Twirling under sunny skies.
With every stroke, a giggle flies,
Creating joy that never dies.

Canvases spin in silly glee,
Where splatters drip like dripping tea.
Art is messy, but that's the charm,
With every blunder, it keeps us warm.

So grab a brush, let's make a mess,
Paint our troubles, and bless the stress.
In this gallery of funny schemes,
Life is but a canvas of dreams.

Luminescent Lines

Lines that shimmer, bounce, and play,
Chasing shadows far away.
Bright as fireflies on a spree,
Dancing vibrantly, wild and free.

Each curve tells a joke or two,
Wiggling like a worm in blue.
They twist and turn with all their might,
Making mischief through the night.

Lines may be silly, lines may be bold,
Crafting tales that must be told.
With laughter echoing in their trails,
They summon joy in whimsical gales.

So let us scribble, let us glide,
On these roads of fun and pride.
For in these twists, so bright and fine,
We find our spark in luminescent lines.

Skylarks of Serenity

Up above, the skylarks sing,
With chirps that make the heart take wing.
They dive and swoop in playful loops,
Dancing with the clouds in joyful groups.

In a world where troubles fade,
They spread laughter like a parade.
Each note is wrapped in sweet delight,
Chasing shadows away from sight.

With feathers bright and spirits high,
They tickle clouds as they fly by.
A serenade of merry tunes,
Painting happiness on the dunes.

So let's join in their cheerful flight,
Embrace the giggles, hold on tight.
For in this space where joy reveals,
We are awash in skylarks' appeals.

Harmonious Journeys

On paths where flutes and laughter blend,
Adventures start and never end.
Each step we take is full of fun,
With quips and jokes we've just begun.

We skip through fields of sugarcane,
Where humor dances in the rain.
Every puddle's a splashy game,
Where silly games ignite the flame.

With melodies that jingle bright,
Together we'll soar, take flight.
Through valleys low and hills so high,
Our hearts will soar, and spirits fly.

So grab your hat, don't miss the show,
We'll roam the world and laugh, you know.
In these harmonious journeys, dear,
We find the joy that brings us cheer.

Whirlwind of Words

Words dance like socks in the dryer,
Spinning and tumbling, oh what a flyer.
They giggle and wiggle, chase one another,
All in a rush, like no word's a bother.

Sentences twist with a cheeky grin,
Puns and jokes ready, let the fun begin.
Adjectives slide, and verbs take a leap,
Whirling around till we've lost track of sleep.

Exclamation marks bounce to the floor,
Commas and periods ready to soar.
In this circus of language, we laugh till we cry,
Juggling our phrases, up high in the sky.

So come join the mayhem, don't be shy,
Let's create a ruckus—oh my, oh my!
Words will take flight, with style and flair,
Together we'll revel, beyond all compare.

Pathways to the Infinite

In the maze of musings, we skip and hop,
Every idea's a door, never a stop.
Tickle your brain with thoughts that are bright,
Paths twisted and turned, what a hilarious sight!

Round every corner, new thoughts come alive,
With giggles and guffaws, we learn how to thrive.
Creative highways stretch far and wide,
Zooming past notions on this whimsical ride.

We chase after dreams with a chuckle and cheer,
Writing down jokes, so deliciously clear.
The map keeps evolving, more twists to be found,
Laughter, our compass, where joy is unbound.

So grab a quill, let your thoughts take flight,
With humor as fuel, the journey feels right.
In pathways of fun, forever we'll roam,
In the land of our laughter, we've truly found home.

Luminescent Lyricism

Shimmering verses, glowing in dark,
Where silly scenarios ignite the spark.
Rhymes dance with delight, like fireflies' glow,
Illuminating the way with laughter's warm flow.

Each line's a twinkle, a humorous sight,
Crafted with care, playful and light.
Metaphors shimmer, a radiant show,
Painting the night with a brilliant flow.

Nonsense collides in a chorus of cheer,
With giggly giggles echoing near.
Verses that sparkle like stars overhead,
Mirthful expressions, where no tear is shed.

So let's twirl around in this vibrant place,
Where lyrics leap and smile with grace.
Join in the fun, let silliness reign,
In luminescent word-play, joy is our gain.

Elevation of Expression

Words climb mountains, take a funny route,
Leaping high up, there's no need to pout.
Each phrase a balloon, floating with glee,
Up, up, and away, come follow with me!

Silly similes race through the air,
Tickling senses, oh what a fair!
Puns soar like eagles, bold and loud,
Expressions elevating, drawing a crowd.

Our thoughts take flight over valleys of joy,
Crafting a symphony without any ploy.
A verbal rollercoaster, twists and surprises,
In the theme park of language, every word rises.

So swing your pen like a kite on the breeze,
Expressing our laughter, aiming to please.
In this elevation, where humor does blend,
We celebrate words, with a giggle to send.

The Art of Ascension

Up we go in a jolly old cart,
With squeaky wheels and a wobbly heart.
Waving at clouds with a cheeky grin,
Who knew that fun could feel like a win?

We bounce and we bob like a fish in a stream,
Chasing silly thoughts, like a happy dream.
Twisting and turning on this joy ride,
Singing tunes that take us for a glide.

Our hats fly off in a whirlwind of joy,
Like balloons that dance, oh what a ploy!
With laughter and giggles, we'll never tire,
As every new twist lights our hearts like fire.

So let's craft our song on this wild ascent,
With silly rhymes and a dash of intent.
We'll reach for the stars with a wink and a dare,
And know that with joy, we'll get anywhere!

Cosmic Cadence

In a rocket ship made of bubblegum,
We sing to the stars, oh what a hum!
Dancing around like a meteor's flight,
Chasing our shadows in the pale moonlight.

Each twinkle of stardust, a note in the air,
We giggle and swirl without a care.
With a wink to the planets, we swirl and sway,
A cosmic ballet that brightens our day.

Aliens join us with their zany tunes,
Playing hopscotch on the bright crescent moons.
We tap to the rhythm of galactic beats,
Stomping our feet in the zero-gravity streets.

As comets zoom past, we holler with glee,
Scribbling memories in the cosmic sea.
Let's ride this wild wave through the endless night,
With laughter and music, oh what a sight!

Melodies in Motion

Wobbling down the street on a pogo stick,
We bounce to the rhythm with a skip and a kick.
With each silly hop, we find our own beat,
Like a marching band made of candy and sleet.

The world is our stage, let the madness erupt,
We'll twirl and we'll leap, oh how we disrupt!
A serenade crafted from giggles and cheers,
As we sway with the breeze and conquer our fears.

With kazoo and tambourine, we make merry sound,
As the laughter we share lifts us off the ground.
In this fun-filled parade, we'll dance till we drop,
Creating sweet melodies, we never will stop!

So join in the fun, let's dance a bit more,
In this whirlwind of joy, we'll all want to soar.
With smiles that sparkle like stars in the night,
We'll make music together, oh what a delight!

Floating Through Metaphors

Drift on a cloud where the giggles reside,
With thoughts like balloons that we all take for a ride.
We balloon up high where imagination shines,
Wrapping our minds in some whimsical lines.

A surf on the breeze with a wink and a cheer,
Let's cram all the sillies in a jar, oh dear!
With a sprinkle of humor, we'll float on a rhyme,
As we dance through the canvas of space and time.

Soaring on puns, we'll never hit ground,
Caught in a whirl of the bright and the sound.
Like candy-floss wishes, we'll color the sky,
While laughter erupts with a snicker nearby.

With metaphors gliding like kites in the sun,
We'll capture the moments and share every pun.
So let's float together on this whimsical ride,
With joy as our compass, we'll take it in stride!

Lyrical Constellations

In a galaxy of song, where laughter swirls,
Jokes float like comets, in sparkly twirls.
A starfish named Fred sings a tune so bright,
While aliens dance under the disco light.

Each note is a planet, spinning with cheer,
A melody crafted from chocolate and beer.
Shooting stars giggle, trailing puns in the sky,
As space cows moo and the rocket chips fly.

On Pluto, they croon with a wobbly groove,
The robot DJ cannot help but move.
In this cosmic jam, the laughter ignites,
With funny-shaped clouds that share silly sights.

So launch your words like balloons in the night,
Let humor and joy be your guiding light.
In this funny universe, let's take a chance,
And sway to the rhythm of a giggly dance.

Palette of the Skies

Buckets of laughter pour from the clouds,
Splashing colors humorous, oh so loud!
A rainbow of giggles, painted with glee,
Where ducks wear top hats and dance on the sea.

Each hue brings a chuckle, a tickle of fun,
The sun wears sunglasses, he's out for a run.
While clouds tell jokes that are silly and bright,
And rainbows play tag with the stars at night.

The breeze carries whispers of witty delight,
As kites wander heaven, soaring in flight.
With crayon-shaped comets, we'll scribble some rhyme,
Creating a canvas of joy out of time.

So grab your brush, let's paint the wide sky,
With cheery confetti, we'll let laughter fly.
In a palette so vivid, we'll find our own song,
In the art of pure fun, where we all belong.

Notes from the Beyond

In the realm of the quirky, notes float around,
As space squirrels gather, with giggles abound.
With a tune made of jellybeans, plinky and loud,
They orchestrate mayhem, a comical crowd.

The echoes of laughter drift far, then come back,
On a comet's tail making a crazy track.
A sketchy old wizard conjures silly spells,
And toads in bowties ring some jingle bells.

With harmonies jumbled and rhythms awry,
The ghosts sing in chorus, their voices all spry.
So tune in to whimsy, hear what they croon,
In the land of the odd, where fun's always noon.

There's magic in giggles, in each little note,
A wacky adventure that makes people float.
So listen closely and you might find,
The silly surprises that dance in your mind.

Celestial Ballads

In the theater of stars, the stage is aglow,
A cast of odd planets put on quite a show.
The moon rolls his eyes at the sun's silly grin,
While martians in tutus prepare to jump in.

Each verse is a comet, with laughs in the tail,
They prance through the cosmos, a vibrant detail.
With space beavers juggling asteroids on high,
And lyrics that bubble like soda nearby.

On mysterious moons, they hum all night long,
With echoes of jokes wrapped in light-hearted song.
The satellites twirl in laughter and cheer,
Their cosmic confetti sprinkles far and near.

So join in the chorus, don't hold back your grins,
Let's sing with the stars, where the fun never ends.
In this whimsical dance, we'll find our own beat,
In celestial ballads, we can't be beat!

Migrations of the Mind

Thoughts take flight, like birds in spring,
Chasing after laughter, what joy they bring.
Wings of whimsy, flutter and sway,
Zooming through dreams, where silliness plays.

Ideas outsmart, like sneaky hares,
Dancing on clouds, with outrageous flares.
Each notion a joke, a comical chase,
A parade of giggles, in endless space.

Synapses wiggle, tickle and tease,
Frolicking fancies drift on the breeze.
A laughably bright, curious spread,
Fueling the fancies that dance in your head.

Surfing on thoughts, like riding a wave,
Riding the chaos, the goofy and brave.
From silly to serious, a somersault spin,
In the carnival of minds, let the fun begin!

Skylight Symphony

A concerto of chuckles, the sun's bright glow,
Conducted by clouds, weaving high and low.
Piano keys sparkle, tickling the skies,
Each note a giggle, where mischief lies.

Rainbow-like laughter paints melodies sweet,
A symphony crafted in the sky's heartbeat.
Instruments of whimsy, starlight and cheer,
Compose a sonata only dreamers can hear.

Trombones are tickles, flutes play a jest,
While bass drums ignite the wild and the best.
Bouncing on breezes, as notes soar above,
A humorous overture, glowing with love.

Join in the harmony, let your mind sway,
In this festival air, where silliness plays.
A tune that erupts in a riotous cheer,
In the skylight's embrace, let laughter appear!

Dreamscapes in Motion

Rolling in laughter, like tumbleweed fun,
Chasing the shadows of everyone's pun.
Flying fish giggle, on a swirl of delight,
Splashing in colors, through day and night.

A trampoline world, where dreams jump and jive,
Each silly thought is a reason to thrive.
Frogs in tuxedos do backflips in glee,
Twisting through fantasties, wild and free.

Dancing with daisies, skimming on air,
Where kites made of jokes shimmer everywhere.
A circus of fancies, attention they steal,
In a carnival world, oh, what a feel!

Wake up from winks, with smiles all about,
In dreamscapes of laughter, let go of your doubt.
Each moment a spark, like fireflies wink,
In the dance of whimsy, just laugh and think!

Aeronautical Arrangements

Up in the air, with balloons full of glee,
Adventure awaits, come sail with me!
Kites of mischief, soar high with finesse,
Silly little setups, need not to impress.

Propellers spinning, with plans so absurd,
Whizzing past clouds, oh, how they've blurred.
Airships of laughter, they float and glide,
In the pockets of joy, let whimsy reside.

Navigating peaks, with maps full of quirks,
Where every turn brings out the work of the jerks.
Clouds whisper secrets in puffs of delight,
In a sky of absurd, everything feels right.

So come take a ride, join the airborne fest,
With laughter as fuel, and humor the best.
An aerial mission, where chuckles reign supreme,
In the skies of nonsense, dare to dream!

www.ingramcontent.com/pod-product-compliance
Lightning Source LLC
Chambersburg PA
CBHW051700160426
43209CB00004B/971